THE MANE EVENT

THE MANE EVENT

HAROLD MORGAN

THE MANE EVENT

© 2020 Harold Morgan

Paperback 978-1-945505-28-7

Kindle 978-1-945505-29-4

Library of Congress data on file with the publisher

Production and publishing services by CMI

Printed in the United States of America

10 9 8 7 6 5 4 3 2 1

CONTENTS

OVERVIEW

The purpose of this book is to show that even though we have a nature animal trait; that when given to God through His word; and through fasting and prayer; you even though your nature find you lost at sometimes; you can still through Christ's help and obedience to God's word through the Spirit; can mature to the type of angel God is asking for! This is what the second coming of Christ is all about! The Mane Event is what the black horses; which represent the black race; is the race, cup and people we're chosen for.

1- INTRODUCTION

The reason I am writing this book is to show that there is an angel that is the second coming of Christ. The second coming of Christ is like the first! There is a person walking right now that will be brought out through the fast. It is also a black figure to lead 144,000 men up in the fast to go into the north country or Mt. Zion.

"Which also said, ye men of Galilee, why stand ye gazing up into heaven? This same Jesus, which is taken up from you into heaven, shall so come in like manner as ye have seen him go into heaven." Acts 1:11

Jesus also said "And other sheep I have which are not of this fold. Them also I must bring, and they shall hear my voice; and there shall be one fold, and one shepherd."

John 10:16

Jesus Christ the same yesterday, today and forever.

Hebrews 13:8

Ezekiel prophecy in chapter 39 verses 21-24. God would set His glory among the heathen, and all the heathen shall see my judgment that I have executed, and my hand that I have laid upon them.

Ezekiel 39:21

So the house of Israel shall know that I am the Lord their God from that day forward. And the heathen shall know that the house of Israel went into captivity for their iniquity; because they trespassed against me, therefore hid I my face from them and gave them into the hand of their enemies. So fell they all by the sword.

Ezekiel 39:22-23

"According to their uncleanness and according to their transgressions have I done unto them, and hid my face from them."

Ezekiel 39:24

Jesus said, "I must work the works of him that sent me while it is day for the night cometh when no man can work."

John 9:4

But an angel will that is why Jesus said, "I Jesus have sent mine angel to testify unto you these things in the churches; I am the root and offspring of David; and the bright and morning star."

Revelation 22:16

The second coming of Christ is Jesus' Angel! Walking on the ground, the angel's name is Lightning!

For as the lightning cometh out of the east and shineth even unto the west; so shall also the coming of the Son of man be.

Matthew 24:27

For as the lightning that lighteneth out one part under heaven, shineth unto the other part under heaven; so shall also the Son of man be in his day.

Luke 17:24

Right now I am praying, stalling for time; that the four angels hurt not any green thing or the sea; till we've sealed the servants of our God in their foreheads! I am rising out of the east with the everlasting gospel. The number sealed was and hundred forty-four thousand, of all the tribes of the children of Israel. *Revelation 7:1-4*

Which we are waiting for the black horse which represents lightning's return bolt. Sealing 144,000 blacks with the name whose father name have understood that it takes 40 days and 40 nights in a row, drinking liquids and eating nothing.

In Revelation chapter ten, the angel has accepted his calling; lifting up his hand and his voice which afterward, seven thunders responded. But he was saying his wrath has become which is the tribulation period. Jesus said, "I beheld Satan as lightning fall from heaven." *Luke 10:18*

We also see that Jesus redeemed lightning's spirit in when he rolled away the stone to open up the tomb for Jesus. Behold there was a great earthquake, for the angel of the Lord descended from heaven and roll back the stone from the door and sat upon it; and his countenance was like lightning; and his raiment white as snow, and for fear of him the keepers did shake, and became as dead men. And the angel answered and said unto the women, fear not ye; for I know that ye seek Jesus, which was crucified. He is not here, for he has risen as he said. Come see the place where the Lord lay, and go quickly and tell his disciples that he is risen from the dead. And behold, he goeth before you into Galilee, there shall ye see him; lo I have told you. *Matthew 28:2-7*

This is the "Mane Event". The engathering of the 144,000 black men to the top of Mt. Zion. Me being the lamb in this hour, leading them 40 days and 40 nights in a row, drinking liquids, without eating solid food at all.

These were not defiled with women, for they are virgins. They were redeemed from among men; being the first fruits unto God and the lamb. These follow the Lamb whithersoever he goeth. Neither was guile found in their mouth. For they are without fault before the throne of God! To have my father's name written in their foreheads.

I heard a voice from heaven as the voice of many waters; I heard a voice of great thunder; a voice of harpers harping with their harps. And they sung as if it were a new song before the four beast and before the elders. And no man could learn that song but the 144,000 which were redeemed from the earth. These follow the lamb where so ever he goeth. *Revelation 14:1-5*

The people the black race will swear and cuss and use foul language. So I swear in my wrath; they shall not enter into my rest. The white horses, which are the white race, will be completely mad at the upset. *Hebrews 3:11*

For these be the days of vengeance; that all things which are written may be fulfilled. But woe unto them that are with child, and to them that give suck in those days! For there shall be great distress in the land and wrath upon this people.

> And they shall fall by the edge of the sword and shall be led away captive into all nations. And Jerusalem shall be trodden down of the Gentiles until the times of the Gentiles be fulfilled.
>
> *Luke 21:22-24*

For I would not brethren that ye should be ignorant of this mystery lest ye should be wise in your own conceits; that blindness in part has happened to Israel, until fullness of the Gentiles be come in. *Romans 11:25*

Right here in the United States, watch for the horse in *Revelation 6:5-6*. The transformation from animal to angel which is lightning in the flesh; will lead the black horse which are the black race in the head to head competition. Winning the triple crown for horses; winning the race, the people and the cup of Christ's sufferings.

> For all that is in the world, the lust of the flesh; the lust of the eyes; and the pride of life is not of the Father but of the world.
>
> *1 John 2:16*

The black horse which is leader of black race; God got black horse to move out of third place overcoming the red horse which is violence. Bolt out in front by fasting; leaving the white horse, and white race, winning the race by at least by eight lengths. Which horse was deception and a lying spirit, which deceived Adam and Eve. He got the crown for that. *Revelation 6:1-2*

> But the last shall be first and the first last; for many be called but few chosen.
>
> *Matthew 20:14*

> But beloved be not ignorant of this one thing that one is with the Lord as a thousand years, and a thousand years as one day.
>
> *2 Peter 3:8*

So Jesus asked for a sign because He drove the money changer, the sheep sellers and them that sold doves out! They asked Him for a sign seeing you are doing this! He answered destroy this temple and in three days I will raise it up! Jesus said to Peter one days is a thousand years and a thousand years with the Lord as one day. *II Peter 3:8*

From Abraham to Christ four thousand years! If a thousand years is as one day we are already into the third day after his death and resurrection, it's now 2019! ! And He said if he tarried no flesh should be saved; but for the elect's sake those days shall be shortened!

God's Angel is already on the ground! Don't look for Him in the sky!! Look for him in the United States this great gentile nation. The temple in Jerusalem will be finished in 2020!! The second coming Christ is here. His angel has been protected to be sure God's plan would come to pass. The night cometh when no man can work. Jesus prophesied about his second image in *Revelation 22:16*.

For all that is in the world; the lust of the flesh, the lust of the eyes; and pride of life is not of the Father; but is of the world!

Some have one; some have two; some have all three! I have two! The lust of the flesh and eyes!

When I see a woman with beautiful titties, nice nipples, nice butt. I undress her with my eyes, I admit! The flesh I am doing better at I am a virgin! No meat whatsoever!! Just like there's a triple crown in the world, there's only one in the spirit. The race, the crown, and the cup. *James 5:16* says "confess your faults one to another and pray ye one for another that ye may be healed the effectual fervent prayer of a righteous man availeth much!

The way to your healing today is to confess to one another; and pray for one another!!

There are only four last spirits in the earth and horsing around in *Zechariah 6:1-8*. The first race to reach the North Country where God dwells are the Black Horses or Race of People. This happens in verse 6 and the white horse which represents the white race go into the North Country after them!! The white race was the favorite in *Revelation 6:1,2;* but will be completely upset by our temper and our foul mouth!!

So we have a foul mouth; but according to *Revelation 7:1-4* and *Revelations 14:1-5* the number of those that were sealed were 144,000 of all the tribes of the children of Israel. We are sealing the black horses which represent the black race; that 40 days and 40 nights drinking, no solid food is the fullness of the Spirit of God, which is Christ. *Romans 8:9*

He started in *1 John 2:15* by saying "Love not the world neither the things which are in the world.

If any man loves the world, the love of the Father is not in him".

> This I say then walk in the Spirit; and ye shall not fulfill the lust of the flesh.
>
> *Galatians 5:16*

When I go empty with no food but just liquids I am in the Spirit. A Spirit doesn't need food. They which do hunger and thirst for righteousness shall be filled. Matthew 5:6

He wasn't just talking drive, but He was talking about literally starving yourself of 40 days and 40 nights no solid food just water or juice. The Belmont

Stakes, The Kentucky Derby, and Preakness, win all three and it's the Triple Crown.

Speaking spiritually the Triple Crown is the victory having gone into the North Country as the first black race. The second leg is the cup of Christ's sufferings through fasting and prayer 40 days and 40 nights. The third leg is the crown of life. This is the only way to kill three birds with one stone.

The pride of life, wanting to gain status in this life, to be rich and famous in this world. I always just wanted enough money to pay my bills.

I will be the first to complete the triple crown; in the head to head competition in *Revelation 6:1-8*.

I am a longshot; and my track record isn't that good. I am bred to win this race, the cup, and the crown. The race is fixed. God's got his pennies which represents deliverance and salvation. *Revelation 6:6*

In this race one victory leads to another test; for growth in Christ. How do we defeat the lust of the eyes? For we walk by faith and not by sight. *II Corinthians 5:7*

> Be not as a horse or mule, which have not understanding, who's mouth must be held in by bit and bridle, lest they come near unto you!
>
> *Psalm 32:9*

God is sovereign He has all the power. He created all things beautiful in its time. The horse is the ideal choice for God; because it has become a race; where winner takes all. Lightning is a closing horse.

The horse is unbeatable on track; if you can get him on track. Which is why the world's favorite being the white horse or the white race. But, God's gotten His choice. The white horse or race is deception and a lying spirit. Which is why he was given a crown; because he tricked Adam and Eve in the garden. God is awarded that black horse or race, which is affliction.

Even though he's a longshot, God will move him from third place to overcome violence the red horse. To first place because we were the first race who fell to sexual intercourse as lightning fall from heaven. *Luke 10:18*

His animal nature is a horse; but his transformation will be the lamb; and his chosen spot closing as an angel in *Revelations 22:16.*

It's down to a two horse race now it's neck and neck in the far turn of the track. The favorite white horse which is the white race will be thrown by our bitter spirit and foul language saying they can't be saved talking like that instead of our people.

Zachariah 6:1-8 verse 6 says calls it the North Country, but it's where the Spirit of God dwells in *Revelations 14:1* I called Mt. Zion. The full fast takes 40 days and 40 nights only liquids, no solid food. A spirit doesn't need food that's why we fast because it ministers unto the Lord. *Acts 13:2*

Fasting means going without solid food, just liquids, clear liquids at that. By not eating you are drawing your spirit back up, along with your soul, to where it was originally. That was the presence of God. No man has ascended up to heaven save that came down from Heaven, even the Son of man, which is in Heaven. That means that if your spirit came down from Heaven at birth, it will return to heaven through Christ. *John 3:13* You will understand that it takes 40 days and 40 nights to reach the presence of God.

In this race, the Mane Event, things just tie into one another. The triple crown is a rare feat to perform in the natural secretariat won it.

I am going to overcome just like God delivered me from almost 20 years of crack cocaine. With God nothing shall be impossible. *Luke 1:37*

God's going to deliver me from every evil work and will preserve me unto His heavenly kingdom. To whom be glory forever and ever and ever amen. *II Timothy 4:18*

The male was supposed to appear before God, three times a year, that worship that's acceptable for a year of God.

Like we said earlier

"For all that's in the world the lust of the flesh; the lust of the eyes; and the pride of life is not the Father but is of the world.

I John 2:16

This leads us into the race's backstretch. Out of the far turn into the lamb in this hour. I am the lamb that gives my life a living sacrifice for 144,000 black men for the triple crown. He has mercy on whom he will have mercy, and on whom he will be hardeneth. *Romans 9:18*

He had mercy on me in Houston, Texas, where I met my first wife I was driving on I-10 from San Antonio. When I reached Houston, someone let me stay with them. When I ran out of jobs needing to put gas in my car the only way I could think of was to pawn the man's TV. A fight broke out later that night because I had to go back to the area; that's all I knew of that part of town.

So the fight moved outside. It was dark, but I sense something on the right I jumped one fence, and that I had made two fences. I fell to the ground saying, "Lord help me."

When I had opened my eyes I was fighting in my sleep; they said at Ben Taub Hospital, "Stop fighting you are alright."

Over $35,000 worth of work was done on me. A "T" was cut in my chest where they opened me up. I had a trach in my neck, weights were on my chest, my right kidney was gone. They said I was dead on arrival and lucky to be alive. I was supposed to go through that; that my body come be in the image that was required!! I had over 150 staples in my chest; which I took out and walked out of the hospital after two weeks.

2 - FAR TURN

Now we're in the far turn!! Where we make the biggest move, I was working on a book in Phoenix, Arizona. I had found a publisher in San Diego. When I got there the Lord said preach it. So I squashed the book.

But now is the time to make a change. In *Zechariah 6:1-8*; we find the four last spirits in the earth. They are all horsing around. The color of the horses is important—it denotes race! The Red Horse is violence in *Revelation 6:3,4*. He was given a sword he takes peace from the earth. They kill one another. The White Horse was given a crown and went forth conquering and to conquer. *Revelation 6: 1,2* said I heard as it were the noise of thunder. This horse is deception and a lying spirit.

The spirit deceived Adam and Eve. So he was given a crown. He's the favorite in Far Turn. In *Revelations 6:5,6* is the Black Horse which is affliction given just enough to sustain him; also God gave him the balance of this race with his 2 pennies down. Affliction is a Closing Horse. And death and hell what can we say they won't win. In *Zechariah 6: 1-8* in verse 6 the Black Horses which represent the black race come first into the North Country which is the presence of God. The White Horses which represent the white race, go forth after them. Revelation 6:8 says they which go into the North Country. 30 days and 30 nights to 40 days and 40 nights without food; just clear liquids.

I am thankful that I am not what I used to be; but I am not all I am going to be. I am yielding more and more to God. Submit yourselves to God, resist the devil and he shall flee from you. *James 4:7*

Like when God delivered me from crack cocaine; while I was trying to steal a tip jar full of money to get high. God showed me I was not controlling the crack the crack was controlling me! I couldn't live with it, and I couldn't live without it. That's when I had my prodigal son moment. I came to myself realizing I did better serving Christ. I came back to my Father; only this time I started fasting and praying and he gave me back my assignment. Which is to lead the black race back to our Father's Spirit and spiritual worship. He showed me I never have to fail again. I can ride this horse to victory! Which is a long way for what I used to think. I used to horse around a lot seeking divers pleasure; taking but not giving. Until I realized I was not walking by faith; I was walking by sight. Whatever I saw that would give me pleasure I went after it. I finally broke free from idolatry, what freedom!!

"Ye shall know the truth and the truth shall make you free".

John 8:32

I am not talking about the baptism in the water; I am not talking about the baptism of the Holy Ghost. I am talking about the baptism of the into Christ. Which means deny yourself food in favor of liquids. I was as far away from God as you could get, but I made a turn far from God to returning to Christ; slowly but surely; one day at a time God put me back in the race. I am sincere this time getting ready to make my way into the backstretch. I am turning from the carnal life (flesh eaters) to vegan. So you see that this race will take another turn in the backstretch.

But now I am fasting this is my second day.

"If we live in the Spirit let us also walk in the Spirit.

Galatians 5:25

I am living without food, just liquids in my system. Not like the former life of idolatry, lust, and iniquity. Follow peace with all men, and holiness without which no man shall see the Lord. *Hebrews 12:14*

I am walking around with nothing but liquids in my stomach until I reach 40 by 40. While I am writing this book, it's a platform of success. I am fasting because the Kingdom of God is not in word but also in power. I *Corinthians 4:20*

I am learning that hereby perceive we the love of God, because He laid down His life for us. We ought to lay down our lives for the brethren. *I John 3:16*

I am coming to you in the Spirit; the love of God will lead you to fast, even though I speak on it. God loves us and when we fast we show God that we love Him because we come to Him with only liquids in our body. No solid food at all. Far Turn is for anyone that has set out to please God where you feel lost out of touch with God; stuck or trapped; or you just don't care. Let me say that God still loves you and still wants to build a relationship with you.

It's not too late. He can catch you no matter how far down you are. That's why he was in the heart of the earth 3 days so the gospel could be preached to the fallen angels; and those that died when Noah's rain killed those people. Fasting and prayer does only what God can do give you the power to become a son of God. You got your body, all you need now is Christ's Paul talking to the Colossians, who said, "this is the mystery that hath been taken from ages and gentiles generations which is

"Christ in you, the hope of glory"

Colossians 1:27

I find that I am more spiritual than religious, which means I am more into the action of spirituality than gathering in a building until I have acquired God's Spirit as a lifestyle.

Some people never get into Christ enough to save themselves; to reach a bonafide son of God. This is what I use to do is lip service; but I have changed me not from the outside; but from the inside out. Draw nigh unto God and He will draw nigh unto you. Cleanse your hands ye sinners and purify your hearts ye double minded. *James 4:18*

There's a huge amount of people at the far turn. If our gospel be hid, it is hid to them that are lost. Whom the God of this world hath blinded the minds of them which believe not lest the light of the glorious gospel of Christ, should shine unto them who is the image of God. *II Corinthians 4:3,4*

I'm an orphan and have never seen my parents. I ended up in Omaha, through Boys Town which I graduated in January of 1975. Before that I was at St. Joseph's Home for Children in Jackson, Michigan. The people said you sound white; I thought to myself what is black. I am black. I started doing everything to conform to the black race. I smoked cigarettes when I saw a white guy blowing smoke rings; I thought that's cool, so I started smoking and coughing because I also had asthma.

I started doing whatever blacks did! Drugs, beer and alcohol. This was the Far Turn for me; everything was acceptable nothing off limits to find out what black meant to me. To fit in to be accepted was my only goal. Even though I started stealing, I realized that riches, money, fame, and power was what I was seeking even though I had a good job.

I wanted a wife. I got married after the incident when I got shot in 1983. We are now coming full circle. I was horsing around again that was the red thread of my life I didn't want to do good. A marriage with 3 kids I left. Two times in jail, both times a flat year with no good time. I cried both times but after the attempted robbery charge which as I said before I got into sin, horsing around happened one last time before I hit my bottom. Almost 20 years in crack cocaine. God broke my will but not my spirit, that's what drove me back to God. That's when the scripture came to me and all this while I was going to church when I felt myself fall off the horse again.

I was ordained as a minister and had a church, but I fell off the horse again, and was back into crack cocaine.

I felt like a failure and let the animal again take me to chaos. Like I said I felt far from God. I was at bottom again. How I would give anything to have sanity, the church was doing well but I let the animal ruin everything. Thinking I could take one hit of crack then have a girl to sex with, but every time I thought I could control it I couldn't until all my money was gone. And every time I wanted I wanted to get high and have sex, I couldn't once it entered into my body I couldn't perform. I think my kidney being gone had a role in this erectile dysfunction. Even without the drugs I can't perform. I think God spared me from the addiction of sex and of getting high. That's when the scripture

"Enter ye in at the strait gate: for wide is that gate, and broad is the way, that leadeth to destruction, and many there be which go threat: Because strait is the gate, and narrow is the way, which leadeth unto life, and few there be that find it."

Matthew 7:13,14

We all have to have boundaries; we all have to set limits for ourselves. I found that quality is better than quantity. When you let your life spiral out of control, you are without morals, guideline and checks and balances; you are I felt that at that time I was the farthest away from God and Christ. Thank you Lord

"He hath mercy on whom He will have mercy; and on whom He will hardeneth"

Romans 9:18

I found my anchor doing the same things over and over again expecting different results is insanity. I couldn't live with it and I couldn't live without it. I had to let go, for if you don't stand for something you'll fall for anything. Going to church where a lot is accepted is not holiness. He said you will find me when you search for me with all your heart. *Jeremiah 29:13*

Now I have sanity in my life; and I follow this scripture, "Seek ye first the kingdom of God and his righteousness and all these things shall be added unto you." *Matthew 6:33*

When I get frustrated and upset, it usually means I am trying to play God, I'm trying to control what's beyond my control.

I made the Far Turn, slowly one day at a time, I am putting my relationship with God first. Now it has been thirteen years since I stopped crack cocaine. I am on Facebook with live broadcast twice a day. I have a prayer service every other Wednesday. I have been the chaplain at the Crown for about 5 years now. Telling my people God has saved us a spot. See *Matthew 26:53* Thinkest that I cannot pray to the Father, He will presently, give me more than 12 legions of angels. I heard the number that were sealed it was 144,000 of all the tribes of Israel. *Revelations 7:4*

We are headed to the Final Turn as we head for the backstretch. The race has taken a turn. The black horses which are the black race has taken a turn. The black horses which are the black race are first in the Final Turn. Which is closely followed by the white horses which are the white race, are second close behind, this race. The black horses which are the black race lightning out in front in the Final Turn. This is going to be a great exciting finish. The red horse went toward the South, not good enough to be picked by God's Christ. The Final Turn is when lightning transform into an angel. Stay close to see if lightning horses around again. He always was the long shot, but chosen by God.

The Final Turn is moving to the chosen spot. Many are called but few are chosen. *Matthew 20:16*

We've worked through the bugs.

"For all that is in the world, the lust of the flesh; the lust of the eyes; and the pride of life; is not of the Father but the world"

1 John 2:16

Some have one, some have two, some have all three. I have two; the lust of the eyes, whenever I see a beautiful girl, nice titties with nipples pointed and a nice butt, I undress her with my eyes, I admit it. I wish all beautiful women were mine. God knows that it's sin, that's why I fast to keep His spirit alive in me. These three culprits have been since the beginning but that white horse which is the white race; in *Revelations 6:1,2* was given a crown he is the early favorite. But that black horse, which is God's leader for the head to head competition.

He will overcome the violence of the red horse in second. Bolt out in front behind his fasting, and take the race, the cup, and the crown; having been first race to appear three times in one year. Which was requirement for all males. The white horse or the white race will be completely upset by the use of our foul language thinking they can't be of God's; but Paul wrote in *Hebrews 3:11*

"So I sware in my wrath, they shall not enter into my rest."

Hebrews 3:11

It takes 40 days and 40 nights in a row to bring Christ into your temple; to become a son of God. The Final Turn is the final piece of the puzzle. I have fasted before; but I didn't see it as a lifestyle. I have to put off eating solid foods instead only liquids in my stomach. Walking around with only clear liquids in my belly; ushering in the Spirit of God; which is the Spirit of Christ. *Romans 8:9*

Paul in *Philippians 3:7, 8* says but what things were gain to me; I counted loss for Christ. "yea, doubtless, and I count all things but loss for the excellency of the knowledge of Christ Jesus my Lord; for whom I have suffered the loss of all things, and do count them but dung; that I might win Christ."

> "Whosoever he be of you that forsaketh not all that he hath, he cannot be my disciple."
>
> *Luke 14:33*

I have lost everything, kids, jobs, shelter, cars, clothes and churches to come to this Final Turn; in which I am becoming the lamb of God for the black race. That their offering up of their bodies as a living sacrifice acceptable to Christ .

We're going around this track in the head to head competition. I have the rainbow of God protection in *Revelation 10*. I am the angel with the little book opened. It was announced by the angel that the tribulation and the day of vengeance has come. Seven thunders uttered their voices which was sealed. This is ushering in the new millennium. Which is the beginning of the Sabbath the 7th day of 7,000 years from Abraham. I am going to go deeper yet. When the day of vengeance is ushered in the falling angels will be able to appear and disappear. Like I said earlier, Solomon Temple is to be finished 2020!

Everything is coming to place on time. It's time for the chaplain to act. The Final Turn is realizing you must sacrifice yourself in the way that God has designed. The Final Turn is about coming full circle; we are in 6,000 years plus; we're into the day of rest. We fast because that is the rest that God is talking about. If you want to be a true worshipper; you have to understand that a spirit doesn't need food that's why while or if you're still carnal; eating flesh you are not in God. When you chose to replace liquids for solid food you're in the temple and in the Spirit of God.

The Final Turn is a choice to move from idolatry to the spirituality that God requires. There are enemies

> "But no weapon formed against you shalt prosper. Every tongue that rises against you in judgment thou shall condemn this is the heritage of the servants of the Lord. Their righteousness is of me sayeth the Lord."
>
> *Isaiah 54:17*

He tried crack cocaine, alcohol, money and fame; to get me to sell out to him instead of Christ. It will never happen. He offered Jesus some things, but he rebuked him according to the Word of God.

When I realized that I had to rely on His Spirit and knowing what His Spirit is I finally stopped horsing around.

The Final Turn is when I completely understood my message, I must live a life that is pleasing to God. Which centers around the holiness of God. There shall be a highway and a way it shall be called the way of holiness. The unclean shall not pass over it. But it shall be for those the way faring men. Though fools shall not err therein. *Isaiah 35:8* This scripture lets us know that there will be a traveler every now and then .

It is so simple that a fool won't be fooled it's so plain. You fast out in the Spirit that gives you the power to do miracles, healings, and the likes.

The Final Turn means the individual has made something finalized; that they will go to the finish.

> They which endure to the end the same shall be saved.
>
> *Matthew 10:22*

You have to make up in your mind; that you are going all the way with God. Christ is the Spirit we need to get. Not the baptism in water; not the baptism of the Holy Ghost; but the baptism into Christ; which only happens because you understand his holiness.

"Be ye holy, for I am holy"

1 Peter 1:16

But the black race has been permitted to use foul language. Does God swear? Yes, He does.

"So I sware in my wrath, they shall not enter into my rest."

Hebrews 3:11

For the great day of his wrath is come and who shall be able to stand.

Revelations 6:17

The black race is going to aide God with pouring out his wrath upon the face of the earth; and them that dwell upon the face of the earth. We are going to move from third to first. We are or I am going to be the first person to go out in the spirit three times in a year since Christ. I have accepted the challenge but God will guide me through the fast to become his angel by transformation through the fast he has sanctified.

The Final Turn is the time when I make my final commitment to go all the way to death, for the name of Christ. Which he has given me the strength to overcome my adversaries. The Final Turn is a complete turnabout in direction. My direction is going the distance with Christ. The distance is 40 and 40 in a row without solid food. I am going to do what no man has done in the church since Christ. I am aware of this challenge after I got clean and freed from crack cocaine.

I have decided to let my body go through the transformation into Christ; which is to submit yourselves therefore to God resist the devil and he will flee from you. Once your body has been purged through fasting the allotted time; joy will be in your soul. Because you have gone the complete time out in the spirit that it takes to purge your soul; becoming that chosen angel to lead the black race to the promise land; which is where the Spirit of God and Christ dwell.

The top of Mt. Zion is where our destination is where the Spirit of God dwells. In the New Testament Mt. Zion, where 144,000 black men are going to let me lead them toward the back stretch. Where we have already dealt with violence the Red Horse. Also, the white race which haven't deceived us because we were the first race that was made last to be first in the end.

3 - BACKSTRETCH

The Backstretch is where the black race; the black horses position themselves for the final stretch. Here we have to stretch ourselves to the total time it takes to acquire the Spirit of God. We are heading back; we have to pace this portion of the race. Coming out of the Final Turn it's a race for the ages. We are coming out of the Final Turn into the Back Stretch; we are exercising ourselves in Godliness. Going up and down, in and out of the Spirit. To exercise my Spirit in fasting and prayer until I can get to full destination 40 days and 40 nights in a row comfortably. I went 40 days and 40 nights in a row twice before; but this is different. I see that it has to be a lifestyle in the Spirit. Going out 2 weeks and then eating one week. Going out 3 weeks, and eating 1 week. Working our way to the top of Mt. Zion. Where is the presence of God dwells? Which is 40 days and 40 nights in a row taking in only liquids. We want to take our system back where it was before. That is where fasting and prayer come in. Who wants to miss a meal, let alone 40 days and 40 nights' worth.

The white race or horses, will have you believe it was only for Jesus: Jesus said I am the way, I am the truth, and I am the Life; no man comes unto the father, but by me. *John 14:6*

We are well into this race and everything is happening according to His word. The Backstretch, is to prove whether you will fast and lengthen your tranquility or not. The Backstretch is where we get the final test that we need moving into the Final Stretch.

> "Ye have need of patience that after ye have done the will of God ye might receive the promise."
>
> *Hebrews 10:36*

While you are fasting for the Lord ye have need of patience one day at a time only drinking liquids that's all. It's a test of your faith; everybody says they want to be like Jesus Christ, but where are the works. Even so faith if it hath not works is dead being alone, yea a man may thou hast faith, and I have works. Show me that faith without thy works, and I will shew you my faith by my works.

James 2:17,18

We are going to back-up in the backstretch; words to encourage you to fast, and move up in God. I know that the works of Christ are missing from the church and or the body of Christ. Jesus said "for without me ye can do nothing" *John 15:5*

This is why I am stressing fasting and prayer;

"For without the Spirit of Christ you are still in the flesh you're none of His."

Romans 8:9

You are still carnal minded if you eat meat.

They that are after the flesh do mind the things of the flesh; but they that are after the Spirit, the things of the Spirit.

Romans 8:5

For to be carnally minded is death; but to be spiritually minded is life and peace.

Romans 8:6

Meats for the belly and the belly for meats, but God shall destroy both it and them.

1 Corinthians 6:13

Meat is one sin that always keeps you out of the temple, that God designs eating meat is called carnality. He said in another place "Touch not the unclean thing and I will receive you." *2 Corinthians 6:17*

Meat gives you a false sense of security, because after you eat, generally you sleep or relax. That's because you're full of meat. From the very beginning, God didn't allow meat at all. Until the days of Noah. But fasting was and always will the one true way to Christ. If you don' t have meat in your body; you are in the temple of God; if you go deeper coming empty to his fullness 40 days and 40 nights eating nothing but liquids.

The distance you die out in the Spirit is the way you rise. If you die 40 days and 40 nights out in the Spirit, you'll receive a full reward. That is why we follow peace with all men and holiness without which no man will see the Lord. *Hebrews 12:14* That's why we walk in peace with all men even our enemies. "For when a man's way please the Lord He maketh even his enemies to be at peace with Him. *Proverbs 16:7* That's why we love one another as yourself; because we want to die out in His fullness 40 days and 40 nights in a row, you go out into the next life with a crown of righteousness.

Why should we back our position because I have the everlasting gospel which I am pouring out on God's people and it is wrath? God is upset with this group of people. No one is about the Father's business. The Backstretch, is about going back into God, and remembering that stretch of time. The Lord let me know He was with me when my ex-wife wanted a divorce but said she didn't have the money. I said if you really want it that bad I will pay for it. So she went down to apply for section 8, the Lord spoke in my spirit you better apply too or you might end up in the streets.

One week later they called and said my name is at the top of the list and we have an apartment for you at the Crown Tower Housing high-rise. It was an awesome miracle because I would have been homeless.

So I moved in, right on time. That was very important to me—having schizophrenia effective disorder; bi-polar type. He put me in position be able to finish out my time here in 2014. Where I became chaplain in 2015. I am presently there, although they cut me from the board for almost two years without a check. But they came back and said we need five people on the board.

They said, "what about the chaplain?" and God moved them to re-elect me. So I started getting a $39.00 check again to present.

I have been having a service every other Wednesday where I use the Daily Bread and make it my message from their message. People in this Crown public high-rise building; accept me now knowing I will do my job without money. Since I been elected and when I wasn't getting a check; I only missed two services. I am beginning to turn up the heat. Through fasting and prayer, I feel the Spirit and in better touch with His spirit. My dream is to publish a book using *Zechariah 6:1-8* as the prophetic anchor of the book. I am in the present tense now. The book I had published wasn't marketed well enough that's why I switched publishers.

This book is about *Zechariah 6:1-8* about the horses as we stated already. The four horses are the last four spirits that dwell upon the face of the earth. Which all are color sensitive black horses represent, the black race; and the white horses represent the white race. There are only two horses remaining in race for the crown. But in *Zechariah 6:1-8* verses 6 says the black race enter into the North Country first and the white race comes in after them. In the end the black race pulls of a great upset. On the white race which had already received a crown for deceiving Adam and Eve in the garden. Because they cuss and use foul language taking the race by upset.

The upset was shocking because their language upset the race (white race). Thinking God doesn't cuss. But is not this true;

> "So I sware in my wrath, they shall not enter into my rest."
>
> *Hebrews 3:11*

Psalms 95:11 says "Unto whom I sware in my wrath; that they shall not enter into my rest" The last two horses are coming through the Backstretch. The angel lightning is the dead carcass, but walking in the Spirit.

"For whosesoever the carcass is thither will the eagles be gathered together."

Matthew 24:28

The angel lightning in *Revelation 10* is the angel with the little book, which John shall swallow; sweet to taste, but bitter in the belly. *Revelations 10:10*

People think that when you cuss or use foul language that you are not in the spirit; but I have two witnesses that God cusses *Hebrews 3:11*and *Psalms 95:11*. God does cuss and swear, because He is upset with those that dwell upon the face of the earth and those that are upon the face of the earth. Which when you understand it means they are in the flesh and not in the Spirit, there are chosen ones that are fasting and truly get it right with God, and that is the black race. Black on black crime will be overcome which is the red horse. The white race shall be overcome by the fasting of the black race especially their leader lightning which lead his race to the promised land, the North country in *Zechariah 6:1-8* verse 6; and the top of Mt. Zion in *Revelations 14:1-5* verse 1.

So far we have covered a stretch; but still we want to cover what the race back is like since we are going through. I am learning to love myself. I am learning that God does really care about me. I am learning to stop feeling sorry for myself. I am learning that I am enough. I am learning how to suit up and show up for myself. God does answer prayers. I am learning to want what I've got. I am learning now to ask for help. I am learning that I count. I am learning my feelings are real and learning to set boundaries. I am learning I am special and there's nobody like me. I am learning to be responsible. I am learning to hold myself accountable. I can be trusted today. I am learning I have what it takes. I am learning to own up to my mistakes. I am learning not to make the same mistakes twice.

I am glad God made me a man. I am learning how to face myself and be objective instead of why me. I say why not me. I am not going to let a problem ruin my whole day. All things work together for good to them that love God; to them who are called according to his purpose. *Romans 8:28*

I am learning I can start my day over any time I want to. I am good looking and love my life and values. I am learning to share with others. I am a good listener; I am learning to hold on to healthy relationships. I am not alone. I am learning to reach out to others and others do matter.

I am gaining ground in the race it is time to move inside. Inside is where the deep truth is. I have always wanted to tell my story if anyone cares to listen. I have a lot to offer; going forward there are going to be obstacles; deeper than the ones before: "God is our refuge and strength a very present help in trouble." *Psalm 46:1*

I always wanted to be able to help; and do something meaningful. It's all inside where the spirit wants to work it's not by might nor by power, but by my Spirit sayeth the Lord of hosts. *Zechariah 4:6*

In the Backstretch you learn there is force beyond that holds all things together. It's that something that you can't explain; a something that brings out the best in you; something beyond reason that lets you know everything is going to be alright. It's that something you can't touch, like the wind but the reality is that its presence is real—it's alive. It calls you from a distance to go beyond what you thought or dreamed of; its right there with you or so you thought it comes and goes. It will lift you like unknown hand then it's silent, it protects you from the unknown. And you wondered why you worried at all. It speaks in a still, small voice. Then you know for sure you were never alone. You thought you had it all figured out, then it was as new as a brand new day. It's that invisible force that's key, then it's a partner invisible, so close you know it's God.

4 - NO CONTEST

We're coming out of the Backstretch to the finish line; it looks like this is No Contest. It's a race for the record book. As one of the greatest races in history. Lightning came out of the Backstretch, bolted out in front moved inside to the rail the rest is history. Lightning won by at least eight lengths no contest from the opening gate he took the lead. In the far turn that white race or horse moved into second place. There was no catching lightning in the backstretch as was mentioned; he bolted out in front increasing his lead then moving inside like a streak to the inside rail the rest is history.

Suffering affliction put him back in third seeming to be a long shot. God put him back on track and groomed him. Seeing the potential; God put in two pennies knowing full well he was a closer. He gets stronger as the race goes on. The Triple Crown, the Belmont Stakes, the Kentucky Derby, and the Preakness. Win all three in the same year is the Triple Crown in horse racing. But in the spirit *1 John 2:16*

"For all that is in the world, the lust of the flesh; the lust of the eyes; and the pride of life is not of the Father, but is of the world."

1 John 2:16

This Triple Crown is equally difficult to do. Lightning made it look easy he was a late entry. But "God doesn't see as a man sees. Man looks on the outward appearance but the Lord looks upon the heart" *1 Samuel 16:7*

The devil is no match, for the Spirit of Christ. He's a loser and always will be. That's what No Contest is about. To show if God's in it, He will win it. He has always come out on top. He doesn't know defeat; He's God all by Himself; and there's no other God beside him. God has fixed the race for the black race to come out on top. The last shall be first and the first last. For many are called, but few chosen. It's No Contest when you use the word.

"Faith cometh by hearing and hearing by the word of God"

Romans 10:17

Even in my life the devil was always had to first face God's spirit; and God holds the future in His hand. I remember when my car overheated when I was headed to San Antonio three people help me push my car in the grass off the ramp I was going to marry this girl I thought. She said she would but she wanted to do it there.

So I went to get some oil and water. When I got back she was nowhere to be found. It was getting dark my car hadn't started yet; here comes the ones that had help. They said when we help we usually get such and such. I knew they were talking about money. I stalling for time said let's go over here if not I will do such and such. They said we're if you're ready. I thought to myself, I'm not going to die out here over little money. So I talked really loudly and said this is all I am giving you three guys $20 a piece; I gave it to them and turn my back and walked, not run to my car and put my head on the steering wheel, then I looked in my mirror 7 of them running at me. I turned the key over the car started I drove off waving goodbye.

Somebody would have said you were lucky; no that was God's protection on my life. I went away praising the Lord. It was nothing short of a miracle revealed to me, that happened. Satan has been trying all the time to thwart God's agenda.

Even when God at first commissioned Moses to say let my people go and did miracles the magicians copied some of the same things Moses and Aaron did. Then they acknowledged God because of what their sorceries couldn't do. God was separating himself as God almighty. Many people today are being fooled by prosperity that all is from God. Satan can also do that he offered Jesus all the kingdoms of the world in a moment of time; and said all would be his if he would fall down and worship him. Jesus answered

"Get you hence Satan; thou shalt worship the Lord thy God and Him only shalt thou serve."

Matthew 4:10

There's no contest if you worship the Living Christ. The thing that separates us are the signs which follow the word.

"And these signs shall follow them that believe, in my name they shalt cast out devils, they shall speak with new tongues. They shall take up serpents, and if they shall drink any deadly thing it will not hurt them; they shall lay hands on the sick and they shall recover. And they went forth and preached everywhere, the Lord working with them, and confirming the word with signs following."

Mark 16:17-20

Yes, there's no contest when fighting against the Lord. I know I was into crack cocaine for almost 20 years the Lord finally broke my will but not my spirit. Now I am going on 14 years clean! And finally I won over the lust of the flesh, the lust of the eyes, and the pride of life "which is not of the Father, but of the world." *1 John 2:16*

I am understanding better

"Love not the world, neither the things that are in the world, if any man love the world, the love of the Father's not in Him."

1 John 2:15

I surrounded myself with good company, I am fasting presently. The Lord may help me in maintaining my sobriety, that's the beginning of my spirituality. Since I came back in 2006, I haven't lost a battle yet. I am keeping my flesh under so I won't look like a castaway.

Spirituality is not for them that need it, it's for them that want it Plenty need it, but plenty don't want it. I was seeking a life of pleasures; divers lusts, and self-centeredness. God knows all of us from the inside out.

"Therefore he hath mercy on whom he will; and whom he will, he hardeneth."

Romans 9:18

Just like Pharaoh he hardened his heart so he could get glory out of Him, and that His name might be declared throughout the whole world. *Romans 9:17*

"I am showing you that with God nothing shall be impossible."

Luke 1:37

It's all according to your faith.

> "If ye abide in me, and my words abide in you, ye shall ask what ye will and it shall be done unto you."
>
> *John 15:7*

In my heart when I was at Boys Town deep within myself I prayed if I get the chance to be one, I'll show 'em how it's done. Now presently I am an example of one that has the Spirit of God.

> "God is not a man, that he should lie, neither the son of man that he should repent, hath he said and shall he not do it? Or hath he not spoken, and shall he not make good?"
>
> *Numbers 23:19*

He's been a rainbow in my life, he has protected me, and preserved me. When I was given my first bible a verse was written it which has been true in my life journey with Christ.

> "Have I not commanded thee? Be strong and of good courage; be not afraid, neither be thou dismayed, for the Lord thy God is with thee whithersoever thou goest."
>
> *Joshua 1:9*

He has been with me whenever in jail twice during my drug days in different parts of the country in different states; he has been there in San Diego, sending a police car my way; when I was about to get robbed made them scatter in the streets. I'm like the man asking healing for his only son. Jesus said if thou canst believe all things are possible to Him that believeth. He said Lord I believe, help thou my unbelief. *Mark 9:24* It's no contest in this fight between good and evil

"Be not overcome of evil, but overcome evil with good."

Romans 12:21

I really try to practice this scripture all the time. Where there's a minus I turn it into a plus. It's possible to never leave out of the temple and go completely liquids.

"For whom he did foreknow he also predestinate (to be) conformed to the image of his son, that he might be the first born of many brethren. It's no contest because of the spirit we are not talking about the baptism in water; or baptism in the Holy Ghost; we're talking about the baptism in Christ. Where you forego solid food in favor of liquids; bringing in the nature of Christ. A full reward is 40 days and 40 nights in a row walking around water in your belly for that same distance.

"What shall he say to these things? If God be for us who can be against us? He that spared not his own son, but delivereth him up for us all; how shall He not with Him freely give us all things?"

Romans 8: 31, 32

"If ye be risen with Christ, seek those things that are above, where Christ sitteth on the right hand of God; set your affections on the above; not on things on the earth."

Colossians 3:1,2

"For by one spirit are we all baptized into one body whether we be Jews or gentiles, whether we be bond or free; and have made to drink into one Spirit."

1 Corinthians 12:13

There's no contest, the black race galloped away forever sealing their fate. This is a reminder of God's awesome power when it comes to the affairs of men. The people's choice the white race couldn't use that same old trick again. We were the first race. The fallen angels mixed the seed with sacrificing children; using our women and mingling the seed. He said, "call upon me in the day of trouble and I will answer thee and shew you great and mighty things which thou knowest not." *Jeremiah 33:3*

You can tell the white horses or race are sore losers and completely upset. The reason it was no contest is they put their trust in the flesh. The black race was granted wisdom how to use their gift of worship. They used deception and got stuck in their own trap. Which when they found out it was too late. It's a lesson for the ages; with God you're more than the world against you. "Your sin shall find you out." *Numbers 32:23*

What can we add to what we've already said; they knew for sure the Lord was with that black race and horse. A testimony for the weary; and hope for the wayfaring man and the traveler alike.

The call is still going out

"Come unto me all ye that labor and are heavy laden; and I will give you rest. Take my yolk upon you and learn of me; for I am meek and lowly in heart. Ye shall find rest unto your souls; for my yolk is easy and my burden is light."

Matthew 11:28-30

In closing I like to thank God; for giving me the ability to write this book Mane Event!!

"But, pray ye that your flight be not in winter, neither on the Sabbath day: For then shall be great tribulation. Such as was not since the beginning of the world to this time, nor ever shall be. And except those days should be shortened, no flesh should be saved; but for the elect's sake those days shall be shortened. Then if any man shall say unto you, lo here is Christ, or there; believe it not. For there shall arise false Christs and false prophets, and shall shew great signs and wonders; insomuch that if it were possible, they shall deceive the very elect. Behold I have told you before."

Matthew 24:20-25

www.ingramcontent.com/pod-product-compliance
Lightning Source LLC
Chambersburg PA
CBHW031634040426
42452CB00007B/821